WHEELS
AT WORK AND PLAY

ALL ABOUT
RACE CARS

For a free color catalog describing Gareth Stevens' list of high-quality children's books, call 1-800-341-3569 (USA) or 1-800-461-9120 (Canada).

Wheels at Work and Play
All about Diggers
All about Motorcycles
All about Race Cars
All about Special Engines
All about Tractors
All about Trucks

Library of Congress Cataloging-in-Publication Data

Flint, Russ.
    All about racecars / Russ Flint.
        p. cm. — (Wheels at work and play)
    Summary: Describes the appearance and power of different types of racing cars.
    ISBN 0-8368-0426-0
    1. Automobiles, Racing—Juvenile literature. [1. Automobiles, Racing.] I. Title. II. Series.
TI.236.F578   1990
629.228—dc20   90-9844

This North American library edition first published in 1990 by
Gareth Stevens Children's Books
1555 North RiverCenter Drive, Suite 201
Milwaukee, Wisconsin 53212, USA

First published in North America by
Ideals Publishing Corporation
565 Marriott Drive, Suite 890
Nashville, Tennessee 37210

Series editor: Tom Barnett
Designer: Laurie Shock

Printed in the United States of America

1 2 3 4 5 6 7 8 9 96 95 94 93 92 91 90

WHEELS
AT WORK AND PLAY

ALL ABOUT
RACE CARS

Russ Flint

Gareth Stevens Children's Books
MILWAUKEE

This Indy car is out of fuel.
It needs new tires.

The pit crew works
very fast.

The formula car is low to
the ground.

This GTP car is painted in bright, flashy colors.

The wheels on a dragster
make smoke.

This pro stock car has an
air scoop.

The GTO goes over
200 miles (320 km) per hour.

This stock car has a "nosepiece" to give it weight.

Sprint cars have "wings."

Midget cars are small.
But they are fast.

This desert racer hits bumps.
It jumps high.

Jeeps are not very
fast. But they
are strong.

Glossary

air scoop
An opening which lets air in to cool the engine.

fuel
A liquid, such as gasoline, that makes the engine run.

nosepiece
A smooth flap which directs air over the front of the car.

pit crew
The people who fix the car and keep it running during the race.

wings
A large piece of metal which helps keep the car from lifting off the ground.

Index

16